Defeat of L.T.T.E by Srilankan
Government proved that Ethnic
Conflict has a military solution.Do you
agree?

Contents

1.Introduction

The world is a home for some 600 crore people. Each individual born in this beautiful earth is entitled for freedom, peace and human rights. People of the African continent may be dark in colour compared to the inhabitants of the west. South Indians may speak and entirely different language from the language spoken in New york. but we all belong to this world, and Our planet belongs to us.

Each individual carries an ethnic identity within him. Ethnicity is not something which divides people, but it differentiates one group from another. But today, it is a sad reality that this ethnic distinctiveness have paved way for unrest and hostility among us. We are discussing this topic in an environment where our motherland is wounded beyond words in a continuous struggle between ethnic communities.

Critics say that conflict between the Tamils and Sinhalese are over for good when Sri lankan Government officially announced that the civil war is over on May 2009,after defeating the Liberation Tigers of Tamil Ealam militarily.

Ethnic conflict can not be solved by defeating a group militarily. Root causes of the ethnic conflict should be resolved to achieve ethnic harmony. We strongly disagree on the Military solution to the Ethnic conflict. It is believed that by defeating L.T.T.E Government has opened a door towards a good solution for Ethnic conflict but ethnic conflicts still prevailing.

Ethnic conflict of Sri lanka is a reality. To resolve this Ethnic conflict, several solutions were forwarded time to time. The Majority was ignorant of these solutions. The LTTE strongly believed in a separate state to resolve the ethnic conflict and they maintained a de facto state. They chose armed struggle to achieve their Goal. It has affected All three communities of Sri lanka.

More than 70,000 Sri Lankans, mostly Tamils, have died since the civil war started in 1983. For 30 years, both the LTTE and the Sri Lankan state have carried out arbitrary arrests, extrajudicial killings, torture, political assassinations and massacres of Tamils, Sinhalese and Muslims.

2. Ethnicity and ethnic conflict

- **What is Ethnicity?**

  Sense of belonging and commitment to a community or group as defined by certain properties such as culture, language, religion, territory or some combination of these and its organizational and operational expressions.

- **What is an Ethnic Conflict?**

An ethnic conflict or ethnic war is a conflict between ethnic groups often as a result of ethnic Nationalism.

A number of scholars have attempted to create the methods available for the resolution, management or transformation of ethnic conflict. John Coakley, for example, has developed a typology of the methods of conflict resolution that have been employed by states, which he lists as: indigenization, accommodation, assimilation, acculturation, population transfer, boundary alteration, genocide and ethnic suicide.

John Mc Garry and Brendan O'Leary have developed a taxonomy of eight macro-political ethnic conflict regulation methods, which they note are often employed by states in combination with each other. They include a number of methods that they note are clearly morally unacceptable.

- Methods for eliminating differences:
  - Genocide
  - Forced mass-population transfers
  - Partition and/or secession (self-determination)
  - Integration and/or assimilation

- Methods for managing differences:
  - Hegemonic control
  - Arbitration (third-party intervention)
  - Cantonisation and/or federalisation
  - Consociationalism or power-sharing

3.Roots of ethnic conflict

Every problem has a root cause. Srilankan ethnic struggle also has an origin. If we would be able to identify and treat the core, we could march towards the solution.

We believe that the starting point of the problem is "power".

Who has the power?, How the power should be delegated, Does the authority who holds power supports injustice?, Does the power belongs to my community?

Always the problem is in an around "Power".

Before colonization Sri Lanka was ruled separately as a blend of kingdoms and Regions by different kings and authorities. The concept of "Power" was different throughout that period. But during the colonization era Sri lanka was brought under one reign and sovereignty. According to the divide and rule policy of Briton, Civil administration accommodated more Tamils and Political administration consisted more Sinhalese.

Therefore both communities started to think about their own power. Disagreements and disputes became apparent. Even after the independence the problem was stagnant and continued to grow into more serious grounds.

We see two sides here.

1. Majority Sinhalese who gained power from the British Colonial masters.

2. Minority communities who were abandoned from the power.

The Majority did not use the power in the appropriate way. They did not use the power to unite people or to grant equal opportunities to all the communities. Instead they used the power to increase the status of Sinhala Language, develop the Livelihood of Sinhala people, encroaching the lands owned by the minority and thus triggering the ethnic unrest. So the instant and foremost reason for the Ethnic conflict in Sri lanka is the improper usage and application of power.

Exploiting the power of the ballot, the majority community of roughly 70 % Sinhala Buddhists has identified itself with the nation, appropriated the state and used it to its own advantage. Ever since independence in 1948, government policies have systematically violated the social, economic and cultural rights of Minorities .

Through the disenfranchisement of the Indian Tamils, through state sponsored colonization of the North-East by Sinhalese settlers, frequently accompanied by forceful eviction of Tamils, through a discriminatory language, education and recruitment policy which pursued but one objective ,the Sinhalization of the state.

Today, more than 90 % of civil servants, and 99 % of the security forces are Sinhalese. The politics of 'positive discrimination' of the Sinhalese appears presently to be transformed into one of long-term exclusion of the Tamils because of proven incapacity.

The surplus of 14 000 Sinhala as against a shortage of 10 000 Tamil medium teachers, the lack of the most elementary school equipment ,a teacher pupil ratio of 70 to 1 in Tamil areas as against 22 to 1 for the rest of the country alone can talk about the continuing discrimination. The results of this outright violation of rights are obvious. In the competitive examinations for the Sri Lanka Accountant and the Administrative Service at most two Tamils were selected each year since the early 1990.Last year in SLAS exams only one Muslim was selected and no Tamils at all.

4. History of Srilankan ethnic conflict

There are different opinions among Historians in when exactly the Ethnic conflict started.

One faction says that it started even before Colonization. Ellalan vs Dutu Gemenu war is often showed as evidence to support.

Another division says that it started during the Colonization period.

Some believe it starts after the Independence.

There are evidences to support all three claims ,thus we find it difficult to verify the exact period.

But more or less we can identify the period where the ethnic conflict was suppressed by violence.1905 Kandy Sinhala Muslim Ethnic conflict was the first recorded communal violence in Sri lanka. but 1983 July riot was the mile stone in the history of the ethnic conflict which eventually gave rise to a military up rise.

Up to 1983

The Sinhalese Kingdoms and Tamil Kingdom in the island were ruled by the Portuguese, Dutch, and even the British, separately till 1833, when for administrative convenience the British combined them and ruled the island as one country. The much quoted Cleghorn Minute of 1799 mentions that two Nations which differed in language, religion and customs occupied the island from ancient times, and detailed their respective boundaries. When the British gave independence they installed a unitary Constitution, handing over the government to the Sinhalese with so-called "entrenched clauses" to safeguard minorities. Sinhalese leaders, who explicitly told Tamils that they would not be discriminated against, deceived them. In fact, the author of that Constitution, Lord Soulbury, later said regretted the fact that he did not implement a federal type of Constitution.

The first agreement on powersharing between the Sinhalese and Tamils was in 1919. This was reneged on by the Sinhalese. There followed another in 1925, which was also reneged by them.

In order to fathom the roots of the conflict between the Sinhalese and Tamils, one has to turn the historical clock back to 1948 when Sri Lanka gained independence from the British.

After independence in 1948, the Sinhalese majority Parliament started to exercise their hegemony and discriminated against Tamils in every sphere of activity, including education, employment and development. The first act of the independent Sri Lankan government was to strip the Tamil plantation workers of the citizenship rights. These workers were descended from people brought to Sri Lanka from India by the British in the 19th century to work on coffee and tea plantations. As a result, at least a million Tamil workers were deprived of Sri Lankan citizenship. About 525,000 of these people were eventually forcefully sent to India.

This hostile act did not completely disenfranchise the other Tamils living in the north and east of the island of Sri Lanka for thousands of years. But soon other laws were pressed into service, which adversely affected the prospects of all Tamils living Sri Lanka. The government made Sinhalese the sole official language rendering people speaking Tamil as second-class citizens. The Tamils were excluded from most government jobs and access to education was denied to them.

The Government set about to change the demography of, primarily, the Eastern province by state-aided colonization. As a result, the percentage of Sinhalese in the Eastern Province increased from a little over 4% in 1924, to a current figure of around 32%. In 1956 legislation was brought to make Sinhalese the only official language. Tamils tried parliamentary methods and Gandhian, non-violent demonstrations to obtain redress. The first communal attacks against Tamils commenced.

A pact was signed in 1957 between Prime Minister Bandaranaike and Tamil leader Chelvanayagm that proposed the establishment of Tamil Regional Councils. This pact was literally torn up in February 1958 due to protests by the other major Sinhalese party - the UNP - and Buddhist priests.

In 1961, following more discrimination and communal attacks, Tamils and Muslims (also Tamil-speaking) carried out a Satyagraha (a non-violent demonstration). The army and police were unleashed on them and their representatives arrested. Tamil areas came under army occupation for the next two years.

In 1965 another pact was signed between the same Tamil leader and the Sinhalese Prime Minister of the other major party, Dudley Senanayake, establishing Tamil District Councils, but this, too, was abrogated in 1968 without being implemented.

At first the Tamils began their peaceful protests against the repression by staging demonstrations, sit-ins and by fighting elections. These demonstrations were met with mob attacks of incited by Buddhist monks and politicians. As no progress could be made to roll back the anti-Tamil policies of the government, the youths increasingly took to violent means to make the government. 'The LTTE was formed in 1972,' notes Chris Lee, 'and carried out its first major armed action in 1978. After the 1983 pogrom, the LTTE gained increased support from the Tamil community and dramatically stepped up its war against the SLA.'

While providing lip service to the fact the country was multiethnic, multicultural multilingual, and, multi-religious, in order to appease the international community, nothing was done towards implementing legislation to satisfy minority aspirations. More discrimination and all kinds of violence affected Tamils. The Federal Party of the Tamils sought and obtained an overwhelming mandate from Tamils to request a federal type of government during this period, to no avail.

In 1972 a new constitution was introduced without the participation of Tamils. It repealed Section 29 of the 1948 Constitution, which was supposed to contain safeguards for minorities, and had been declared by the British Privy Council to have entrenched clauses, which were supposedly unalterable. The new constitution also abolished the second chamber (the Senate) and appeals to this Privy Council. It gave primary place to Buddhism.

In 1976 the Tamils, as a last resort, gave their representatives an overwhelming mandate to ask for separation.

In the run up to the 1977 general elections Mr. Jayawardena outlined the problems suffered by the Tamils very eloquently, saying "so much so that they have asked for separation," and promised to solve the problems of the Tamils. His party got a landslide victory capturing 7/8th of the seats. Rather than solving the national or ethnic problem, he set about establishing an Executive Presidential system and became the first such President. A new Constitution was passed giving more prominence to Buddhism. Again Tamil representatives did not participate in the drawing up of the 1978 Constitution.

The LTTE was proclaimed a terrorist organization in 1978, and in 1979 a Prevention of Terrorism Act (PTA) was enacted. The PTA was called "the worst regulation introduced in any civilized country including South Africa' by international jurist Paul Seigart.

1979 to 1983 saw the declaration of an emergency in Tamil areas, military occupation of the Jaffna Peninsula, burning of shops, arbitrary arrests of youth, rape, torture and killing, burning of the Jaffna Public Library, looting and burning of the business district, and island-wide riots against Tamils. The army was given the power to shoot and bury without holding a coroner's inquest.

The worst pogrom took place in 1983 when over 3-4,000 Tamils were killed and 95% of the property owned by Tamils outside their areas was destroyed. Tamil political prisoners were killed in prison and Tamils fled as refugees by shiploads to the Tamil homelands.

The war called Eelam War 1 started

The Sinhala majority ruled with policies that discriminated against Tamils. Tamils were killed

in planned campaigns between 1956 and 1983.
Sinhala became the sole official language. Tamils
had to obtain higher marks than Sinhalese in order
to get into university. And, Tamil voices were
excluded from the political sphere. Government-
sponsored Sinhala settlements were set up in
Tamil areas-and when the LTTE killed several
Sinhala settlers, many Tamils were massacred.

1983 to 2002

Tamil militancy reached a new height in response
to the anti-Tamil planned campaign of 1983 when
an estimated 2,000 to 3,000 Tamils were
butchered, torched or beaten to death at the hands
of Sinhala mobs. But in 1986, the LTTE began
eliminating other militant Tamil factions that had
also formed to stand up to the Sri Lankan state.
They massacred Tamils who did not support
them, claiming sole representation of Tamils. In
1990, they expelled an estimated 75,000 Muslims
from northern Sri Lanka. They also massacred 75
Muslims returning from pilgrimage, 120 Muslims

at prayer in a mosque at Kattankady, and another 120 in the village of Eravur.

1987

1987 July 29: India-Sri Lanka Peace Accord (aka Rajiv-Jayewardene Accord) signed in Colombo, followed by the induction of Indian army in Sri Lanka as Indian Peace Keeping Force (IPKF).

1987 Aug. 4: After returning to homeland from India, LTTE leader Prabhakaran addressed a mammoth meeting held at Suthumalai, Jaffna. He declared that 'We are surrendering our arms to the Indian army relying on the basis of assurances given by the Indian Prime Minister Rajiv Gandhi.'

1987 Aug.18: A bomb attack targeting the top leaders of UNP within parliament premise when the UNP parliamentary group meeting was in progress. One deputy minister was killed and 10 were injured, including the Minister of National Security Lalith Athulathmudali.

1987 Sept. 15: Thileepan, the LTTE political leader of Jaffna district, began a fast unto death over five demands made to the Indian government. Thileepan's fast took place in front of Nallur Kanthaswamy temple.

1987 Sept.26: Thileepan attained martyrdom at 10:48 am. The representatives/diplomats of the Indian government ridiculed Thileepan's death.

1989 April 12: President Premadasa announced a unilateral ceasefire between SL armed forces and LTTE. In turn, LTTE rejected this ceasefire offer noting 'Until the Indian army of Oppression leaves our land, there will be no such thing as a ceasefire.'

1989 May 4: First meeting between President Premadasa and LTTE representatives Anton Balasingham, Adele Balasingham, Yogaratnam Yogi and Paramu Murthy.

1989 May 5: First round of Talks between GOSL representatives and LTTE. The talks continued until May 28th. The chief representative of GOSL team was A.C.S.Hameed, the prominent Muslim Cabinet minister.

1989 June 2: President Premadasa forwarded a letter to Indian primeminister Rajiv Gandhi urging him to withdraw the IPKF by July 31st, the 2nd anniversary of IPKF induction.

1989 June 15: Second round of Talks between GOSL representatives and LTTE began.

1989 June 20: Indian primeminister Rajiv Gandhi responded to President Premadasa's withdrawal request, with diplomatic demands of discussions on mutually agreed schedule for IPKF, and for full implementation of the July 1987 Accord, insisting that both should be 'parallel exercises'.

1990

1990 March 24: The last troops of IPKF left Sri Lanka.

1990 October 30th Forcible eviction of Northern Muslims by LTTE

1991

1991 May 21: Rajiv Gandhi, the Indian prime minister from 1984-89, was assassinated at Sriperumbudur, ahead of his anticipated address at Congress Party election rally. The assassin was tagged as 'Dhanu' (a human bomb) by the Indian law enforcement officials. 18 people (that included Rajiv's security detail, police personnel and 'Dhanu') in the vicinity also died in the bomb blast.

1993 May 1: President Premadasa was killed in Colombo while engaged in working the assembled crowd in the party's May Day rally. The assassin was described by the police and press as a suicide bomber who barged into President's security cordon in a bicycle. Within hours, vital forensic evidence of the killing had been destroyed by the organizers of the rally.

1994 Nov.9: 3rd Executive Presidential election. Chandrika Kumaratunga leading PA defeated Sirima Dissanayake (UNP), in a landslide (62%). who was nominated as a replacement of her assassinated husband Gamini Dissanayake.

1994 Nov.12: Chandrika Kumaratunga took oath as the 4th Executive President.

1995 Apr. 19: Eelam War III (between GOSL and LTTE) began.

1997

1997 May 13: *Operation Jayasikuru* (Victory Assured) launched by the GOSL in the northern Tamil homeland. LTTE, under the overall command of Prabhakaran, resisted GOSL army, with commanders Balraj, Sornam, Karuna, Anbu, Bhanu and Jeyam. The A-9 trunk road linking Jaffna and Kandy was the theater of this Operation.

1999 Dec.18: President Chandrika Kumaratunga was wounded in an eye at an SLFP election rally in Colombo. At a UNP election rally in Ja-ela, a Colombo suburb, Major General Lakshman (Lucky) Algama was assassinated.

1999 Dec. 22: Fourth Presidential election held. Chandrika Kumaratunga (People's Alliance) polled 4,312,157 votes (51.5%) against Ranil

Wickremasinghe (UNP) 3,602,748 votes (42.7%) and was elected for the second time.

2000

2000 Oct.10: 11th General Elections held for the Sri Lankan parliament.

2000 Dec.21: As a gesture of goodwill, LTTE unilaterally declared a month-long ceasefire, effective Christmas Eve, December 24th.

2000 Dec.23: GOSL rejected LTTE's ceasefire and asserted that military offensives against LTTE would continue.

2001

2001 Jan.24: LTTE extended the unilateral ceasefire and called on the International Community to persuade GOSL to reciprocate favorably and kick-start the negotiation process.

2001 Feb.22: LTTE extended the unilateral ceasefire by another month and called on the International Community again to persuade the GOSL to reciprocate favorably to its goodwill measure.

2001 Mar.22: LTTE extended the unilateral ceasefire until April 24th and warned that they would resume armed operations if GOSL refused to reciprocate the ceasefire and continues its military operations against the LTTE.

2001 Apr.23: After a 4 month-long ceasefire, LTTE called off its unilaterally imposed restraint.

2001 Apr.24: Within hours of LTTE terminating its unilaterally declared ceasefire, GOSL forces launched a massive military campaign (Operation Agni Keela aka Fire Ball). Operation *Agni Keela* turned out to be a debacle to GOSL.

2001 July 24: LTTE cadres infiltrated the Katunayake air base and destroyed 13 air crafts including two Kfir jet fighters, one MI-24 Helicopter gun ship and one MIG-27- jet fighter in blitzkrieg style.

2002

2002 Feb.22: The Ceasefire Agreement (CFA) was signed between GOSL and LTTE, with Norway as the chief facilitator.

2002 Sept.16-18: The 1st Session of direct peace talks between GOSL and LTTE held in Thailand.

2002 Oct.31-Nov.3: The 2nd Session of peace talks between GOSL and LTTE held in Thailand.

2002 Dec.2-5: The 3rd Session of peace talks between GOSL and LTTE held in Oslo, Noway.

2002 to 2009

- ✓ Ranil –Praba Agreement (2002) MOU

- ✓ Oslo Peace Talks (2002)

- ✓ ISGA by LTTE (2004)

- ✓ in March 2004 there had been a major fracturing between the northern and eastern wings of the LTTE. Colonel Karuna, the Eastern commander of the LTTE and one of Prabhakaran's trusted lieutenants, pulled 5,000 eastern cadres out of the LTTE, claiming insufficient resources and power were being given

to Tamils of the eastern part of the
island.

✓ June 24 2004 , the government and
LTTE agreed on the Post-Tsunami
Operational Management Structure (P-
TOMS), but it received sharp criticism
from the JVP, who left the government
in protest. The legality of P-TOMS
was also challenged in the courts.
President Kumaratunga eventually had
to scrap P-TOMS, which led to
widespread criticism that sufficient aid
was not reaching the North and East of
the country.

✓ Sri Lankan Foreign Minister
Lakshman Kadirgamar, a Tamil who
was highly respected by foreign
diplomats and who had been sharply
critical of the LTTE, was assassinated
at his home on August 12, 2005,
allegedly by an LTTE sniper .His

assassination led to the marginalization of the LTTE from the international community.

✓ Geneva Peace Talks – (2006)

✓ 2006 again LTTE broke up from MOU and start (4th Elam war)

2009 May, it was announced that the armed struggle had come to an end finally.

The defeat of Liberation Tigers of Tamil Eelam on or around May 17, 2009, marked the end of Eelam War 4 and the complete domination of Eelam by the Singhalese dominated Sri Lanka government. Two and a half decades of Tamil armed resistance thus came to an end. The Tamils, before the armed rebellion started, had been subjected to repeated racial attacks by the Singhalese mobs and armed forces. It culminated in 1983, when around 3,000 Tamils were massacred throughout the country, and 90 % of their property in Singhalese majority areas destroyed. Non violent agitation by Tamils for over 35 years was brutally crushed by the Singhalese.

The entire LTTE leadership were killed or captured by the triumphant Singhalese armed forces. The defeat of the Tamil Tigers sent shock waves throughout the Eelam Tamil nation within and outside Sri Lanka. While it was known that LTTE was retreating and cornered, Tamils did not expect the LTTE to give up the fight. LTTE in the conduct of the war, committed the blunder of taking the civilians with them on their retreat, even when cornered in Mullaitivu. This made it possible for the Sri Lankan government to intern the surrendering Tamil civilians of about 300,000 in concentration camps behind barbed wires and armed Singhalese guards. The innocent Tamils thus fell from the frying pan into the fire.

5.Outcome of the armed struggle

War casualties

Minister of Defence Gotabhaya Rajapaksa said on an interview with state television that 23,790 Sri Lankan military personnel were killed since 1981 (it was not specified if police or other non armed forces personnel were included in this particular figure).

From the August 2006 recapture of the Mavil Aru reservoir until the formal declaration of the cessation of hostilities (on May 18), 6261 Sri Lankan soldiers were killed and 29,551 were wounded[

The Sri Lankan military estimates that up to 22,000 Tamil Tiger rebels were killed in the last three years of the conflict

The United Nations has released an estimate on the number of people killed in Sri Lanka's 27 year civil war.

The UN's humanitarian co-ordination office says 80,000 to 100,000 people were killed in the war between the government and Tamil Tiger rebels.

Crush down of the non violence struggle to find a solution for ethnic conflicts

It is one year since the Sri Lankan government declared 'victory over terrorism'. However, efforts in finding a long-term political settlement to the ethnic issue is nowhere in sight. Presently, the top priority of the Rajapaksa regime seems to be 'development' and not ethnic reconciliation. The sole aim of the present UPFA government under Mahinda Rajapaksa is to make Sri Lanka the 'Singapore of South Asia'. What is therefore required in their belief is a stable government under a strong leader and devoid of any 'external interference'. Using near-two-thirds majority obtained in the recently concluded parliamentary elections, various steps are being taken in this regard.

First, the plan is to amend the Constitution to

remove two-term cap on the President so that Rajapaksa can continue beyond 2017; and second, to further entrust him with more powers. Other changes in the pipeline are instituting a Senate (second chamber) at the national level and a change in the electoral system – from proportional representation to first-past-the-post system or a mix of both. The Sri Lankan President has also appointed an eight-member Commission on 'Lessons Learnt and Reconciliation' (LLRC) to pre-empt the United Nations' move to appoint an experts panel on 'war crimes' during the last stages of war.

Economic crisis

- The cost of Sri Lanka's four-year war on terrorism from 2006-2009 amounted to 5.5 billion US dollars according to, Ajith Nivard Cabraal the governor of the Central Bank.

	1982	1983	1985	1988	1990	1993	1994	1995	1996
Defense expenditure as a % of total government expenditure	3.1	4.4	10.2	14.3	14.6	14.7	15.2	18.1	21.6
Defense Budget as a % of GDP	1.1	1.4	3.5	4.8	4.5	4.2	4.4	5.4	6

Sources: Central Bank of Sri Lanka. Review of the Economy and Annual Report, various issues.

6.Why military solution is destructive?

Genocide of an entire ethnic community- Mostly the ethnic conflict demolished by military action one ethnic group is completely destroyed.

War leaves scars that can never be healed.

Armed struggle is over but these questions remains unanswered.

1. What will happen to the Tamils in the pemanant concentration camps in East, Vanni and North?

2. How extent will the military zone be expanded and swallow even more tamil traditional lands?

3. Who will monitor no further Sinhala colonization, demographical changes in the Minority traditional lands?

4. Who will take account of the war crimes committed?

7.Recommended Solutions for the conflict

- The Sri Lankan military has desecrated the holy ashes of an elderly lady ,Prabhakaran's mother in North.
- This is not Buddhism in Sri Lanka (this is barbarism).
- Sri Lankan President keeps mum over desecration of Holy Ash

These were the headlines which hit the News papers this February 22nd .

Network of exiled Sri Lankan journalists and human rights defenders, expresses its serious concern about the incident. The ashes of a cremated mother had been desecrated and the bodies of three dogs killed by shooting were thrown into the cremation spot. In accordance with the Hindu tradition, the ashes of a cremated body are collected the next day to be dissolved in a river or sea. According to media reports the ashes had been scattered by military vehicles running over the spot. NFR sources in Jaffna confirmed the truth of this incident and indicated that no one wants to speak about it openly because of fear.

Sri Lankan government controls the television and radio stations that have the broadest outreach in the country, but also to undermine the integrity and the credibility of organizations—human rights organizations, journalist organizations—by raising claims, allegations of embezzlement, fraud, malpractice, you know, completely tarnishing individuals, targeting individuals. And I think there's been—the threat to the freedom of expression and opinion has been accompanied by a threat to the freedom of association.

If the present condition prevails then in two years time the Tamil race will be thing of the past in Sri Lanka, Kayal alias Angayarkanni said to TruthDive, who was detained in Sri Lanka recently for visiting the northern part of the island nation. An advocate by profession, along with her associate M Thirumalai, Kayal had visited the Tamil regions in Sri Lanka, including Vavunia, Mattakalappu, Omandai, Kilinochi, Jafna and Valvettithurai and got to know firsthand the condition of the Tamils in various camps.

She said that a camp at Kattariankulam in Vavunia had 1600 Tamil. Most of them were women and men who were less in number were without a hand or a foot. The healthy men who were LTTE soldiers are put in torture camps and those injured are put in centers for internally displaced, the relief materials did not reach the affected. She said that around 9000 young men who are healthy are kept in torture centers.

Around 16000 women are still in the camps she said. According to Kayal the women are subjected to sexual harassment. Only thirty percent of the relief work reaches the camps. The UN team was given petitions by numerous mothers to ask the Sri Lankan Government to trace out their missing sons. Agricultural tools meant for the Tamils were used by the Sinhalese, she pointed out.

Kayal and Thirumalai are functionaries of Naam Tamilar Party. They were allegedly detained by the Lankan Army. Only after the intervention of the Prime Minister office was the duo released.

While the LTTE is unlikely to recover its former strength, it can be expected that it continue to operate in other forms such as the influence of the Tamil diaspora However, Sri Lanka's core problem remains unsolved - the island's Tamil minority feels like second-class citizens.

The government is now confining Tamil civilians from the former LTTE-controlled areas of northern Sri Lanka in camps to discover rebels among them. Reports of human rights abuses by the army have emerged from those facilities, access to which the government has blocked and which critics refer to as 'concentration camps.'

The camps are certain to reinforce the Tamils' impression that they are being discriminated against in their homeland. It was this feeling that gave rise to the LTTE in the first place.

The 'Four-Ds' strategy – Demilitarisation, Development, Democratization, and Devolution – in that order of priority has been reiterated by President Rajapaksa. The government is still in the first two phases and says the others "will follow at a later stage." Colombo has been articulating the need for finding a 'home grown solution' to the ethnic issue.

However, at the maximum, what is on the cards is the existing 13th Amendment, an offshoot of the Indo-Sri Lanka Accord of 1987. Through the 13th Amendment, the island was divided into various provinces and granted some powers under Provincial List. However, the Provincial Councils always lacked sufficient powers – especially land, police and finance – to run their affairs in an efficient manner. In addition, the Centre wields immense powers of overruling any Provincial decisions. Instead of strengthening the Provinces, the present government is planning to dilute the present arrangement further. Unless there is genuine power sharing, the Provincial Council arrangement will be mere eyewash.

The Rajapaksa government also has to go beyond the constitutional tinkering in reaching out to minorities by showing generosity of spirit. Resettlement of the displaced, reconstruction of the war- destroyed northeast and rehabilitation of the LTTE cadres should be done in a more serious and fair manner. Trust insufficiency that exists between various communities of the island must be bridged on a priority basis. These confidence building measures will go a long way in convincing even the Tamil diaspora that is presently keeping the hopes of Tamil Eelam alive. It is important for the Sri Lankan government to engage the diaspora to make them contribute positively to the development of the country.

In our view according to the theory that each problem has a solution, there is a solution for the ethnic conflict our country. A solution which benefits the entire nation is the best and greatest solution. Any solution without the following basis would be invalid.

1. Reality of the problem must be understood

2. Background knowledge of the people and the environment which it is going to be implemented.

3. Resources to be used when implementing the solution

4. Ideological changes

5. Attitudinal changes

6. Flexibility

7. Continuous maintenance

As a our problem is unique the solution should be exclusive. We don't need to copy paste any solution. Let us forget the arguments on whether it should be a federal system, provincial system ,unilateral system or any other system. We should go for a localized solution with the equal participation of Sinhalese, Tamils and Muslims forgetting all other differences. We believe that any possible solution should start from the grassroot level and not from the top tp bottom. If we can guarantee the equal contribution of all the ethnic groups we can walk towards eternal peace in Sri lanka.

08.Conclusion

LTTE or not, Prabhakaran or not, the root cause of militant uprising is due to the genuine political grievances of the Tamil minority. For long they have been subjugated as second class citizens, under representation in the political decision making process and a silent alienation of the culture.Of course all of these might sound diffused complaints but they are real.

The numerous peace accords and treaties signed by the Sri Lankan government have not helped the Minority population mollify their grievances.

As long as the Minorities are oppressed, Sri Lanka will never be able to live in peace.

We believe that by defeating L.T.T.E Government has opened a door towards a good solution for Ethnic conflict. It is agreed that LTTE was a big obstacle towards the long road of PEACE. By defeating them Militarily President Mahinda

Rajapakse has opened a road towards Ethinic Harmony. If we think that we can suppress the voice of Tamil speaking community by defeating LTTE militarily, we are wrong.

It will be an opening to another war.

Works cited.

Jayantha Perera, "Political Development and
Ethnic Conflict in Sri Lanka," *Journal of Refugee
Studies,*
Vol 5, No 2 (1992): pp. 136-148.

Bruce Matthews, "Radical Conflict and the
Rationalization of Violence in Sri Lanka," *Pacific
Affairs,*
Vol. 59. No 1 (Spring 1986): 28-44.

Mahinda Rajapakse: A man of the masses,
http://www.mahindarajapaksa.com.

Ilankai Tamil Sangam- Association of Tamils of
Sri Lanka in the US http://www.sangam.org/

Tens of Thousands attend Tamil resurgence event
Killinochchi,http://www.tamilnet.com/art.html?ca
tid=13&artid=15759.

http://en.wikipedia.org/wiki/Sri_Lankan_Civil_War

WWW Virtual Library Sri Lanka
http://www.lankalibrary.com/pol2.html

THE SRI LANKAN TAMIL DIASPORA
AFTER THE LTTE- Asia Report N°186 – 23
February 2010
Ground views – Journlaism for citizens,
http://groundviews.org/2008/04/29/what-is-the-
solution-to-the-ethnic-conflict-in-sri-lanka/

www.ingramcontent.com/pod-product-compliance
Lightning Source LLC
Chambersburg PA
CBHW070448290526
45791CB00005B/2095